Contents

Planet Earth	4
The Sun	6
Day and night	8
The Moon	10
Moving Moon	12
The Solar System	14
The Universe	16
Space travel	18
See it yourself!	20
Glossary	22
Quiz	23
Answers and Index	24

The words in **bold** can be found in the glossary.

Planet Earth

We all live on Earth. Earth is a **planet**. It is **surrounded** by space.

Earth is the only planet that people live on.

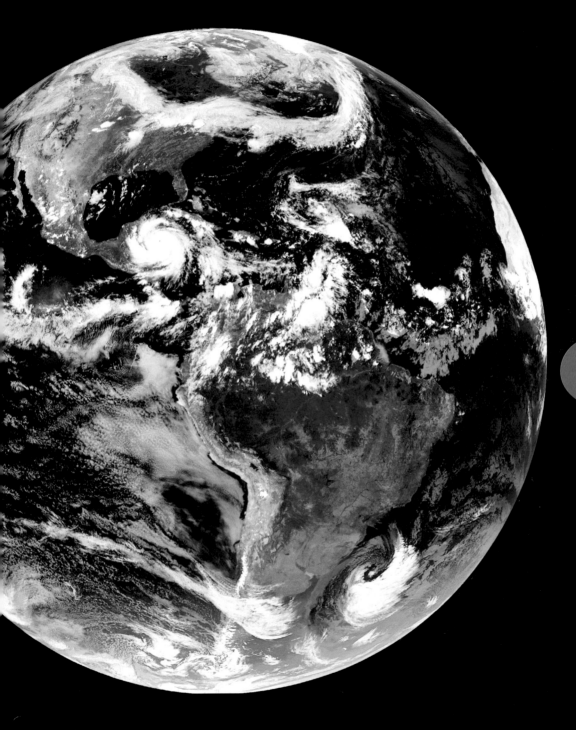

5

The Sun

The Sun is a big, bright **star**. Although it is very far away, it gives us light and heat here on Earth.

The Sun helps crops to grow.

Day and night

We have day and night because Earth slowly spins around. When our part of Earth faces the Sun, we have daylight.

The Sun is very bright. Never look directly at it.

The Moon

At night, we can see the Moon in the sky. The Moon does not give out light itself. It is lit by the Sun.

From Earth, the Moon looks different each night.

Moving Moon

The Moon goes around or **orbits** Earth. It takes 27 days to completely orbit Earth.

The Moon is made of grey rock.

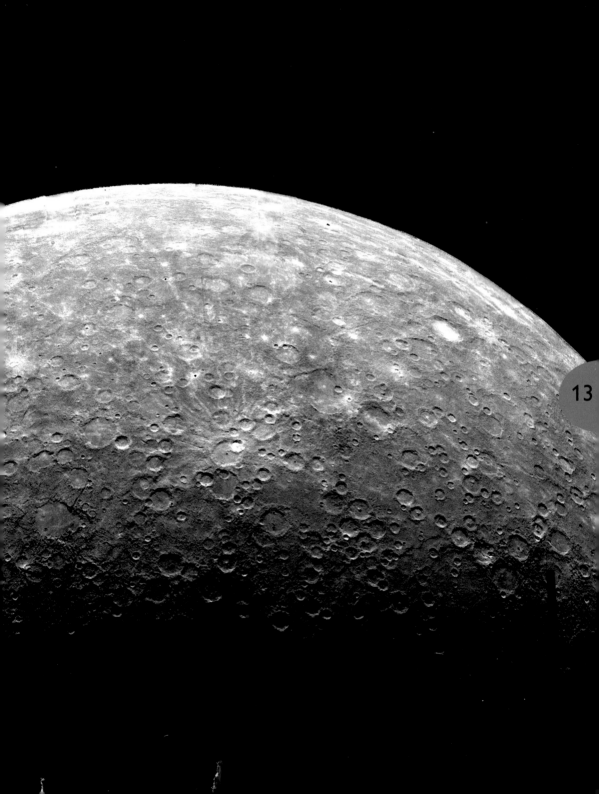

Neptune

Saturn

Uranus

Mars

Venus

Jupiter

14

Earth

Mercury

The Solar System

Earth, the Sun and
the Moon are part
of the **solar system**.
Earth and the seven
other planets in the
solar system orbit
the Sun.

The planets are Mercury,
Venus, Earth, Mars, Jupiter,
Saturn, Uranus and Neptune.

The Universe

The solar system is part of the **Universe**. The Universe is huge. It contains billions of stars and planets.

The Universe is bigger than we can imagine!

space travel

Space is hard to explore. **Astronauts** have visited the Moon. It took them three days to get there!

Astronauts have driven around the Moon in a buggy.

See it yourself!

One day, we may be able to travel all over space. Until then, we can look at it through a **telescope**!

We can look at the planets at night.

Glossary

Astronaut - someone who travels in space

Orbit - to go around something

Planet - a huge, round object in space

Solar system - the Sun and all the planets and moons that go around it

Star - a huge, burning ball of gas in space

Surround - to be all around something

Telescope - a tool used to make things that are far away seem closer

Universe - the whole of space, including all the stars, planets and moons

Websites:

http://www.kidsastronomy.com

http://www. nasa.gov/audience/forkids/kidsclub/flash/

index.html

Quiz

Use the information in the book to answer these questions.

1.   Which is the only planet that people live on?

2.   What is the Sun?

3.   How long does the moon take to orbit Earth?

4.   Can you name three planets in the solar system?

5.   What can we use to look at space?

(The answers are on page 24.)

Answers

1. Earth
2. A star
3. 27 days
4. (Any of) Mars, Jupiter, Saturn, Venus, Mercury, Neptune, Uranus or Earth
5. A telescope

Index

astronauts 18–19

Earth 4–5, 7, 8, 15

Moon 10–11, 12–13, 15, 19

planets 4, 15, 20

space 4, 20

solar system 14–15, 17

Sun 6–7, 8, 11, 15

telescope 20

Universe 16–17